easy
Soups

easy

Soups

LOVE FOOD

Love Food ® is an imprint of Parragon Books Ltd

Parragon
Queen Street House
4 Queen Street
Bath BA1 1HE, UK

Photography by Clive Bozzard-Hill and Mike Cooper
Food styling by Carol Tennent, Val Barrrett, Carol Handslip, and Sumi Glass
Introduction by Anne Sheasby

ISBN 978-1-4075-6799-0

Printed in Indonesia

NOTES FOR THE READER

- This book uses imperial, metric, and US cup measurements. Follow the same units of measurement throughout; do not mix imperial and metric.
- All spoon measurements are level: teaspoons are assumed to be 5 ml, and tablespoons are assumed to be 15 ml.
- Unless otherwise stated, milk is assumed to be lowfat and eggs are medium. The times given are an approximate guide only.
- Some recipes contain nuts. If you are allergic to nuts you should avoid using them and any products containing nuts.
- Recipes using raw or very lightly cooked eggs should be avoided by infants, the elderly, pregnant women, convalescents, and anyone with a chronic condition.

Contents

Introduction

Soups are appealing in so many ways because they are versatile, easy to prepare, and are full of flavor and goodness, making them a nutritious and satisfying choice. Soups can be served as a first course, a light meal, or a snack, and the more substantial hearty soups can be served as a meal in themselves.

Rich and warming soups are ideal for chilly fall or winter days, chilled soups are perfect for summer dining al fresco, wholesome soups are a good choice for a filling lunch or supper, and light, delicate soups provide an appetizing start to a dinner party or family celebration.

Homemade Soups

Soups can be made using many different ingredients and are perfect for making the most of seasonal produce. Typically, most soups are savory, but some (often sweet) fruit-based soups are also popular in some countries. When making soup, using a good-quality, well-flavored stock is key to creating a really delicious soup.

Good, homemade stocks are preferable, but if you are short of time, choose from an improved range of stock products available on the market, including chilled fresh stock, bouillon powder, or concentrated liquid stock. Alternatively, save the cooking water when boiling or steaming vegetables and add it to soups instead of some or all of the stock, for extra flavor.

Some soups are served chunky-style, while many are served all or partly puréed, so when making soup at home, a blender or food processor (or a hand-held stick blender) will prove to be a real bonus. A large, preferably heavy pan is also ideal for cooking soup.

Small dumplings and small pasta (known as pastina or "soup pasta") add substance to some soups, and ground almonds or oatmeal can be stirred into soup to thicken, enrich, and add flavor and texture.

Many soups freeze well, providing an ideal stand-by for when you have less time to prepare and cook a meal. Single servings of soup can also be frozen in small individual containers for convenience. Simply remove the soup from the freezer and thaw it, then reheat it gently, but thoroughly, until hot.

Croûtons & Other Accompaniments

Plenty of fresh crusty bread or bread rolls, served warm or cold, is often the only accompaniment a soup needs, but alternative choices such as croûtons, melba toast, bruschetta, and garlic bread will equally enhance even the simplest of soups.

Croûtons (small cubes of crisp, golden fried bread) add a lovely finishing touch to a wide variety of puréed soups, adding extra flavor, crunch, and appeal. Croûtons can be made from many types of plain bread, including white, whole wheat, or multigrain, as well as from flavored breads such as sun-dried tomato, olive, herb, or cheese breads.

Bread slices can also be cut into different mini shapes rather than small squares to make the croûtons more attractive. Try tossing the hot croûtons in chopped fresh herbs or freshly grated Parmesan, or sprinkle them with ground spices to add extra flavor and appeal.

Garnishing Soup

Garnishes provide the decorative finishing touch to many soups and they should look attractive and complement the flavors of the soup. A sprinkling of chopped fresh parsley or snipped fresh chives may be all that is required. A swirl or two of cream, crème fraîche, or plain yogurt in the center of each serving looks lovely, especially if it is then feathered with a toothpick or skewer. Top with a sprinkling of finely chopped scallions, crumbled crispy bacon, or a sprinkling of paprika, chili powder, or black pepper to add the finishing touch.

Small sprigs of fresh herbs such as thyme, basil, rosemary, or parsley sprigs also look great. A light sprinkling of finely grated or thinly shaved hard cheese such as fresh Parmesan or cheddar, or a little crumbled bleu cheese, adds extra delicious flavor to many soups.

For a slightly more elaborate garnish, top each portion with a spoonful of pesto or herb pistou (similar to pesto)—ideal for tomato or vegetable soups—and swirl it in just before serving. A drizzle of olive, chili, or sesame oil works really well as a garnish on some soups and thinly pared fruit zests such as shreds of orange or lemon suit other soups.

Vegetable Stock

Makes: about 8¾ cups

Ingredients

2 tbsp sunflower or corn oil

scant ½ cup finely chopped onion

scant ½ cup finely chopped leek

⅔ cup finely chopped carrots

4 celery stalks, finely chopped

¾ cup finely chopped fennel

1 small tomato, finely chopped

10 cups water

1 bouquet garni

Heat the oil in a large pan. Add the onion and leek and cook over low heat, stirring occasionally, for 5 minutes, until softened. Add the remaining vegetables, cover, and cook for 10 minutes. Add the water and bouquet garni, bring to a boil, and simmer for 20 minutes.

Strain the stock into a bowl, let cool, cover, and store in the refrigerator. Use immediately or freeze in portions for up to 3 months.

Fish Stock

Makes: about 5⅔ cups

Ingredients

1 lb 7 oz/650 g white fish heads, bones, and trimmings, rinsed

1 onion, sliced

2 celery stalks, chopped

1 carrot, sliced

1 bay leaf

4 fresh parsley sprigs

4 black peppercorns

½ lemon, sliced

5⅔ cups water

½ cup dry white wine

Cut out and discard the gills from any fish heads, then place the heads, bones, and trimmings in a saucepan. Add all the remaining ingredients and gradually bring to a boil, skimming off the foam that rises to the surface. Partially cover and simmer for 25 minutes.

Strain the stock without pressing down on the contents of the strainer. Leave to cool, cover, and store in the refrigerator. Use immediately or freeze in portions for up to 3 months.

Chicken Stock

Makes: about 11¼ cups

Ingredients

3 lb/1.3 kg chicken wings and necks

2 onions, cut into wedges

17½ cups water

2 carrots, coarsely chopped

2 celery stalks, coarsely chopped

10 fresh parsley sprigs

4 fresh thyme sprigs

2 bay leaves

10 black peppercorns

Put the chicken wings and necks and the onions in a large pan and cook over low heat, stirring frequently, until lightly browned.

Add the water and stir well to scrape off any sediment from the base of the pan. Gradually bring to a boil, skimming off the foam that rises to the surface. Add all the remaining ingredients, partially cover, and simmer for 3 hours.

Strain the stock into a bowl, let cool, cover, and store in the refrigerator. When cold, remove and discard the layer of fat from the surface. Use immediately or freeze in portions for up to 6 months.

Beef Stock

Makes: about 7½ cups

Ingredients

2 lb 4 oz/1 kg beef marrow bones, cut into 3-inch/7.5-cm pieces

1 lb 7 oz/650 g braising beef in a single piece

12½ cups water

4 cloves

2 onions, halved

2 celery stalks, coarsely chopped

8 black peppercorns

1 bouquet garni

Place the bones in the base of a large pan and put the meat on top. Add the water and gradually bring to a boil, skimming off the foam that rises to the surface.

Press a clove into each onion half and add to the pan with the celery, peppercorns, and bouquet garni. Partially cover and simmer for 3 hours. Remove the meat and simmer for 1 hour more.

Strain the stock into a bowl, let cool, cover, and store in the refrigerator. When cold, remove and discard the layer of fat from the surface. Use immediately or freeze in portions for up to 6 months.

1

Vegetarian

Tomato Soup

serves 4

- 1/4 cup butter
- 1 small onion, finely chopped
- 1 lb/450 g tomatoes, coarsely chopped
- 1 bay leaf
- 3 tbsp all-purpose flour
- 2 1/2 cups milk
- salt and pepper
- sprigs of fresh basil, to garnish

Melt half the butter in a pan. Add the onion and cook over low heat, stirring occasionally, for 5–6 minutes until softened. Add the tomatoes and bay leaf and cook, stirring occasionally, for 15 minutes, or until pulpy.

Meanwhile, melt the remaining butter in another pan. Add the flour and cook, stirring constantly, for 1 minute. Remove the pan from the heat and gradually stir in the milk. Return to the heat, season with salt and pepper, and bring to a boil, stirring constantly. Continue to cook, stirring, until smooth and thickened.

When the tomatoes are pulpy, remove the pan from the heat. Discard the bay leaf and pour the tomato mixture into a food processor or blender. Process until smooth, then push through a fine strainer into a clean pan. Bring the tomato purée to a boil, then gradually stir it into the milk mixture. Season to taste with salt and pepper. Ladle into warmed bowls, garnish with basil, and serve immediately.

Leek & Potato Soup

serves 4–6

¼ cup butter

1 onion, chopped

3 leeks, sliced

8 oz/225 g potatoes, cut into ¾-inch/2-cm cubes

3½ cups vegetable stock

salt and pepper

⅔ cup light cream, to serve (optional)

2 tbsp snipped fresh chives, to garnish

Melt the butter in a large saucepan over medium heat, add the onion, leeks, and potatoes, and sauté gently for 2–3 minutes, until softened but not browned. Pour in the stock, bring to a boil, then reduce the heat and simmer, covered, for 15 minutes.

Transfer the mixture to a food processor or blender and process until smooth. Return to the rinsed-out saucepan.

Reheat the soup, season with salt and pepper to taste, and serve in warmed bowls, swirled with the cream, if using, and garnished with chives.

Chunky Vegetable Soup

serves 6

2 carrots, sliced

1 onion, diced

1 garlic clove, crushed

12 oz/350 g new potatoes, diced

2 celery stalks, sliced

4 oz/115 g white mushrooms, quartered

14 oz/400 g canned chopped tomatoes

2½ cups vegetable stock

1 bay leaf

1 tsp dried mixed herbs or 1 tbsp chopped fresh mixed herbs

½ cup corn kernels, frozen or canned, drained

2 oz/55 g green cabbage, shredded

freshly ground black pepper

sprigs of fresh basil, to garnish (optional)

Put the carrots, onion, garlic, potatoes, celery, mushrooms, tomatoes, and stock into a large pan. Stir in the bay leaf and herbs. Bring to a boil, then reduce the heat, cover, and let simmer for 25 minutes.

Add the corn and cabbage and return to a boil. Reduce the heat, cover, and simmer for 5 minutes, or until the vegetables are tender. Remove and discard the bay leaf. Season to taste with pepper.

Ladle into warmed bowls, garnish with basil, if using, and serve immediately.

Minestrone

serves 4

2 tbsp olive oil

2 garlic cloves, chopped

2 red onions, chopped

1 red bell pepper, seeded and chopped

1 orange bell pepper, seeded and chopped

14 oz/400 g canned chopped tomatoes

4 cups vegetable stock

1 celery stalk, trimmed and sliced

14 oz/400 g canned cranberry beans, drained

3½ oz/100 g green leafy cabbage, shredded

2¾ oz/75 g frozen peas, thawed

1 tbsp chopped fresh parsley

2¾ oz/75 g dried vermicelli

salt and pepper

freshly grated Parmesan cheese, to garnish

Heat the oil in a large saucepan over a medium heat, add the garlic and onions and cook, stirring, for 3 minutes, until slightly softened. Add the red and orange bell peppers and the chopped tomatoes and cook for an additional 2 minutes, stirring. Stir in the stock, then add the celery, cranberry beans, cabbage, peas, and parsley. Season with salt and pepper. Bring to a boil, then lower the heat and simmer for 30 minutes.

Add the vermicelli to the pan. Cook for another 10–12 minutes, or according to the directions on the package. Remove from the heat and ladle into serving bowls. Garnish with freshly grated Parmesan and serve immediately.

EASTER SEALS 2011

Chilled Red Pepper & Orange Soup

serves 4

5 blood oranges

3 tbsp olive oil

3 lb 5 oz/1.5 kg red bell peppers, seeded and sliced

1½ tbsp orange flower water

salt and pepper

extra virgin olive oil, for drizzling (optional)

Finely grate the rind of one of the oranges and shred the rind of another with a citrus zester. Set aside. Squeeze the juice from all the oranges.

Heat the oil in a pan, add the red bell peppers and cook over medium heat, stirring occasionally, for 10 minutes. Stir in the grated orange rind and cook for an additional few minutes. Reduce the heat, cover, and simmer gently, stirring occasionally, for 20 minutes.

Remove the pan from the heat, let cool slightly, then transfer the red pepper mixture to a food processor and process to a smooth purée. Add the orange juice and orange flower water and process again until thoroughly combined.

Transfer the soup to a bowl, season with salt and pepper to taste, and let cool completely, then cover with plastic wrap and chill in the refrigerator for 3 hours. Stir well before serving sprinkled with the shredded orange rind and drizzled with extra virgin olive oil, if using.

French Onion Soup

serves 6

1 lb 8 oz/675 g onions

3 tbsp olive oil

4 garlic cloves, 3 chopped and 1 halved

1 tsp sugar

2 tsp chopped fresh thyme, plus extra sprigs to garnish

2 tbsp all-purpose flour

½ cup dry white wine

8½ cups vegetable stock

6 slices French bread

10½ oz/300 g Gruyère cheese, grated

Thinly slice the onions. Heat the oil in a large, heavy-bottom pan over medium-low heat, add the onions, and cook, stirring occasionally, for 10 minutes, or until they are just beginning to brown. Stir in the chopped garlic, sugar, and chopped thyme, then reduce the heat and cook, stirring occasionally, for 30 minutes, or until the onions are golden brown.

Sprinkle in the flour and cook, stirring constantly, for 1–2 minutes. Stir in the wine. Gradually stir in the stock and bring to a boil, skimming off any foam that rises to the surface, then reduce the heat and simmer for 45 minutes.

Meanwhile, preheat the broiler to medium. Toast the bread on both sides under the broiler, then rub the toast with the cut edges of the halved garlic clove.

Ladle the soup into 6 ovenproof bowls set on a baking sheet. Float a piece of toast in each bowl and divide the grated cheese among them. Place under the broiler for 2–3 minutes, or until the cheese has just melted. Garnish with thyme sprigs and serve immediately.

Cream of Pea Soup

serves 4

4 tbsp butter
1 onion, finely chopped
1 lb/450 g shelled peas
1/2 cup water
2 1/2–3 cups milk
salt and pepper

Melt the butter in a pan over low heat. Add the onion and cook, stirring occasionally, for 5 minutes until softened.

Add the peas and pour in the water. Increase the heat to medium and simmer for 3–4 minutes, or until the peas are tender. (Frozen peas will be ready in 10 minutes.)

Add 2 1/2 cups of the milk, season with salt and pepper, and then bring to a boil, stirring continuously.

Remove the pan from the heat and let cool slightly, then pour the soup into a food processor and process to a smooth purée.

Return the soup to the rinsed-out pan and bring back to a boil. If the soup seems too thick, heat the remaining milk in a small pan and stir it into the soup. Taste and adjust the seasoning if necessary, and serve.

Gazpacho

serves 4

9 oz/250 g white bread slices, crusts removed

1 lb 9 oz/700 g tomatoes, peeled and chopped

3 garlic cloves, coarsely chopped

2 red bell peppers, seeded and chopped

1 cucumber, peeled, seeded, and chopped

5 tbsp extra virgin olive oil

5 tbsp red wine vinegar

1 tbsp tomato paste

9½ cups water

salt and pepper

4 ice cubes, to serve

Tear the bread into pieces and place in a blender. Process briefly to make breadcrumbs and transfer to a large bowl. Add the tomatoes, garlic, bell peppers, cucumber, olive oil, vinegar, and tomato paste. Mix well.

Working in batches, place the tomato mixture with about the same amount of the measured water in the food processor or blender and process to a purée. Transfer to another bowl. When all the tomato mixture and water have been blended together, stir well and season to taste with salt and pepper. Cover with plastic wrap and chill in the refrigerator for at least 2 hours, but no longer than 12 hours.

When ready to serve, pour the soup into chilled serving bowls and float an ice cube in each bowl.

Creamy Mushroom & Tarragon Soup

serves 4–6

3 tbsp butter

1 onion, chopped

1 lb 9 oz/700 g white mushrooms, coarsely chopped

3½ cups vegetable stock

3 tbsp chopped fresh tarragon, plus extra to garnish

⅔ cup sour cream

salt and pepper

Melt half the butter in a large pan. Add the onion and cook gently for 10 minutes, until soft. Add the remaining butter and the mushrooms and cook for 5 minutes, or until the mushrooms are browned.

Stir in the stock and tarragon, bring to a boil, then reduce the heat and simmer gently for 20 minutes. Transfer to a food processor or blender and process until smooth. Return the soup to the rinsed-out pan.

Stir in the sour cream and add salt and pepper to taste. Reheat the soup gently until hot. Ladle into warmed serving bowls and garnish with chopped tarragon. Serve at once.

Vegetable Soup with Pesto

serves 6

1 tbsp olive oil

1 onion, finely chopped

1 large leek, thinly sliced

1 celery stalk, thinly sliced

1 carrot, quartered and thinly sliced

1 garlic clove, finely chopped

6¼ cups water

1 potato, diced

1 parsnip, finely diced

1 small kohlrabi or turnip, diced

5½ oz/150 g French beans, cut into small pieces

5½ oz/150 g fresh or frozen peas

2 small zucchini, quartered lengthwise and sliced

14 oz/400 g canned cannellini beans, drained and rinsed

3½ oz/100 g spinach leaves, cut into thin ribbons

salt and pepper

jar of basil pesto

Heat the olive oil in a large saucepan over medium-low heat. Add the onion and leek and cook for 5 minutes, stirring occasionally, until the onion softens. Add the celery, carrot, and garlic and cook, covered, for an additional 5 minutes, stirring frequently.

Add the water, potato, parsnip, kohlrabi, and french beans. Bring to a boil, reduce the heat to low, and simmer, covered, for 5 minutes.

Add the peas, zucchini, and cannellini beans and season generously with salt and pepper. Cover again and simmer for about 25 minutes until all the vegetables are tender.

Add the spinach to the soup and simmer for an additional 5 minutes. Taste and adjust the seasoning and stir about a tablespoon of the pesto into the soup. Ladle into warmed bowls and serve with any remaining pesto.

Tuscan Bean Soup

serves 6

- 10½ oz/300 g canned cannellini beans, drained and rinsed
- 10½ oz/300 g canned cranberry beans, drained and rinsed
- 2½ cups vegetable stock
- 4 oz/115 g dried conchigliette or other small pasta shapes
- 4 tbsp olive oil
- 2 garlic cloves, very finely chopped
- 3 tbsp chopped fresh flat-leaf parsley
- salt and pepper

Place half the cannellini and half the cranberry beans in a food processor with half the stock and process until smooth. Pour into a large, heavy-bottom pan and add the remaining beans. Stir in enough of the remaining stock to achieve the consistency you like, then bring to a boil.

Add the pasta and return to a boil, then reduce the heat and cook for 15 minutes, or until just tender.

Meanwhile, heat 3 tablespoons of the oil in a small skillet. Add the garlic and cook, stirring constantly, for 2–3 minutes, or until golden. Stir the garlic into the soup with the parsley.

Season to taste with salt and pepper and ladle into warmed soup bowls. Drizzle with the remaining olive oil and serve immediately.

Creamy Carrot & Parsnip Soup

serves 4

4 tbsp butter
1 large onion, chopped
1 lb/450 g carrots, chopped
2 large parsnips, chopped
1 tbsp grated fresh ginger
1 tsp grated orange zest
2½ cups vegetable stock
½ cup light cream
salt and pepper
sprigs of fresh cilantro, to garnish

Melt the butter in a large pan over low heat. Add the onion and cook, stirring, for 3 minutes, until slightly softened. Add the carrots and parsnips, cover the pan, and cook, stirring occasionally, for about 15 minutes, until the vegetables have softened a little. Stir in the ginger, orange zest, and stock. Bring to a boil, then reduce the heat, cover the pan, and simmer for 30–35 minutes, until the vegetables are tender. Remove the soup from the heat and let cool for 10 minutes.

Transfer the soup to a food processor or blender and process until smooth. Return the soup to the rinsed-out pan, stir in the cream, and season well with salt and pepper. Warm through gently over low heat.

Remove from the heat and ladle into soup bowls. Garnish each bowl with pepper and a sprig of cilantro and serve.

Watercress Soup

serves 4

- 2 bunches of watercress (about 7 oz/200 g), thoroughly cleaned
- 3 tbsp butter
- 2 onions, chopped
- 8 oz/225 g potatoes, coarsely chopped
- 5 cups vegetable stock or water
- whole nutmeg, for grating (optional)
- salt and pepper
- ½ cup crème fraîche, yogurt, or sour cream, to serve

Remove the leaves from the stalks of the watercress and set aside. Coarsely chop the stalks.

Melt the butter in a large saucepan over medium heat, add the onions, and cook for 4–5 minutes, until soft. Do not brown.

Add the potatoes to the saucepan and mix well with the onions. Add the watercress stalks and the stock.

Bring to a boil, then reduce the heat, cover, and simmer for 15–20 minutes, until the potato is soft.

Add the watercress leaves and stir in to heat through. Remove from the heat and transfer to a food processor or blender. Process until smooth and return the soup to the rinsed-out saucepan. Reheat and season with salt and pepper to taste, adding a good grating of nutmeg, if using.

Serve in warmed bowls with the crème fraîche spooned on top with an extra grating of nutmeg, if desired.

Spiced Pumpkin Soup

serves 4

2 tbsp olive oil

1 onion, chopped

1 garlic clove, chopped

1 tbsp chopped fresh ginger

1 small red chile, seeded and finely chopped

2 tbsp chopped fresh cilantro

1 bay leaf

2 lb 4 oz/1 kg pumpkin, peeled, seeded, and diced

2½ cups vegetable stock

salt and pepper

light cream, to garnish

Heat the oil in a pan over medium heat. Add the onion and garlic and cook, stirring, for about 4 minutes, until slightly softened. Add the ginger, chile, cilantro, bay leaf, and pumpkin, and cook for another 3 minutes.

Pour in the stock and bring to a boil. Using a slotted spoon, skim any foam from the surface. Reduce the heat and simmer gently, stirring occasionally, for about 25 minutes, or until the pumpkin is tender. Remove from the heat, take out the bay leaf, and let cool a little.

Transfer the soup into a food processor or blender and process until smooth (you may have to do this in batches). Return the mixture to the rinsed-out pan and season to taste with salt and pepper. Reheat gently, stirring. Remove from the heat, pour into warmed soup bowls, garnish each one with a swirl of cream, and serve.

Roasted Squash, Sweet Potato & Garlic Soup

serves 6–8

1 sweet potato, about 12 oz/350 g
1 acorn squash
4 shallots
2 tbsp olive oil
5–6 garlic cloves, unpeeled
3¾ cups vegetable stock
½ cup light cream
salt and pepper
snipped chives, to garnish

Preheat the oven to 375°F/190°C.

Cut the sweet potato, squash, and shallots in half lengthwise, through to the stem end. Scoop the seeds out of the squash. Brush the cut sides with the oil.

Put the vegetables, cut-side down, in a shallow roasting pan. Add the garlic cloves. Roast in the preheated oven for about 40 minutes, until tender and light brown.

When cool, scoop the flesh from the potato and squash halves, and put in a saucepan with the shallots. Remove the garlic peel and add the soft insides to the other vegetables.

Add the stock and a pinch of salt. Bring just to a boil, reduce the heat, and simmer, partially covered, for about 30 minutes, stirring occasionally, until the vegetables are very tender.

Allow the soup to cool, then transfer to a food processor or blender and process until smooth, working in batches if necessary.

Return the soup to the pan and stir in the cream. Season with salt and pepper, and then reheat. Ladle into warmed bowls, garnish with snipped chives and serve.

Spinach & Cheese Soup

serves 6–8

- 8 oz/225 g fresh baby spinach leaves, tough stalks removed
- 2½ cups milk
- 3 cups vegetable stock
- scant 1 cup cream cheese flavored with garlic and herbs
- salt and pepper
- croûtons (optional)

Put the spinach in a large pan and pour in the milk and stock. Bring to a boil, then reduce the heat and simmer gently for 12 minutes. Remove the pan from the heat and let cool completely.

Ladle the cold soup into a food processor, in batches if necessary, and process until smooth. Cut the cheese into chunks and add to the soup. Process again until smooth and creamy.

Pour the soup into a bowl and season with salt and pepper to taste. Cover with plastic wrap and let chill in the refrigerator for at least 3 hours. Stir well before ladling into bowls. Add croûtons, if using, and serve immediately.

Sweet Potato & Bleu Cheese Soup

serves 4

4 tbsp butter

1 large onion, chopped

2 leeks, trimmed and sliced

6 oz/175 g sweet potatoes, peeled and diced

3½ cups vegetable stock

1 tbsp chopped fresh parsley

1 bay leaf

⅔ cup heavy cream

5½ oz/150 g bleu cheese, crumbled

pepper

2 tbsp finely crumbled bleu cheese, to garnish

thick slices of fresh bread, to serve

Melt the butter in a large pan over medium heat. Add the onion and leeks and cook, stirring, for about 3 minutes, until slightly softened. Add the sweet potatoes and cook for another 5 minutes, stirring, then pour in the stock, add the parsley and the bay leaf, and season with pepper. Bring to a boil, then lower the heat, cover the pan, and simmer for about 30 minutes. Remove from the heat and let cool for 10 minutes. Remove and discard the bay leaf.

Transfer half of the soup into a food processor and blend until smooth. Return to the pan with the rest of the soup, stir in the cream, and cook for another 5 minutes. Gradually stir in the crumbled cheese until melted (do not let the soup boil).

Remove from the heat and ladle into serving bowls. Garnish with finely crumbled cheese and serve with slices of fresh bread.

2

Fish & Shellfish

Bouillabaisse

serves 4

- scant ½ cup olive oil
- 3 garlic cloves, chopped
- 2 onions, chopped
- 2 tomatoes, seeded and chopped
- 2¾ cups fish stock
- 1¾ cups white wine
- 1 bay leaf
- pinch of saffron threads
- 2 tbsp chopped fresh basil
- 2 tbsp chopped fresh parsley
- 7 oz/200 g live mussels
- 9 oz/250 g snapper or monkfish fillets
- 9 oz/250 g haddock fillets, skinned
- 7 oz/200 g shrimp, peeled and deveined
- 3½ oz/100 g scallops
- salt and pepper

Heat the oil in a large pan over medium heat. Add the garlic and onions and cook, stirring, for 3 minutes. Stir in the tomatoes, stock, wine, bay leaf, saffron, and herbs. Bring to a boil, reduce the heat, cover, and simmer for 30 minutes.

Meanwhile, soak the mussels in lightly salted water for 10 minutes. Scrub the shells under cold running water and pull off any beards. Discard any mussels with broken shells or any that refuse to close when tapped. Put the rest into a large pan with a little water, bring to a boil, and cook over high heat for 4 minutes, or until the mussels open. Remove from the heat and discard any that remain closed.

When the tomato mixture is cooked, rinse the fish, pat dry, and cut into chunks. Add to the pan and simmer for 5 minutes. Add the mussels, shrimp, and scallops and season with salt and pepper to taste. Cook for 3 minutes, until the fish is cooked through. Remove from the heat, discard the bay leaf, and ladle into serving bowls.

Salmon & Leek Soup

serves 4

1 tbsp olive oil

1 large onion, finely chopped

3 large leeks, including green parts, thinly sliced

1 potato, finely diced

2 cups fish stock

3 cups water

1 bay leaf

10½ oz/300 g skinless salmon fillet, cut into ½-inch/1-cm cubes

⅓ cup heavy cream

fresh lemon juice (optional)

salt and pepper

sprigs of fresh chervil or parsley, to garnish

Heat the oil in a heavy-bottom saucepan over medium heat. Add the onion and leeks and cook for about 3 minutes until they begin to soften.

Add the potato, stock, water, and bay leaf with a large pinch of salt. Bring to a boil, reduce the heat, cover, and cook gently for about 25 minutes until the vegetables are tender. Remove the bay leaf.

Allow the soup to cool slightly, then transfer about half of it to a food processor or blender and process until smooth. (If using a food processor, strain off the cooking liquid and reserve. Purée half the soup solids with enough cooking liquid to moisten them, then combine with the remaining liquid.)

Return the puréed soup to the saucepan and stir to blend. Reheat gently over medium-low heat.

Season the salmon with salt and pepper and add to the soup. Continue cooking for about 5 minutes, stirring occasionally, until the fish is tender and starts to break up. Stir in the cream, taste, and adjust the seasoning, adding a little lemon juice if desired. Ladle into warmed bowls, garnish with chervil or parsley, and serve.

Thai-Style Seafood Soup

serves 4

5 cups fish stock

1 lemongrass stalk, split lengthwise

pared rind of ½ lime, or 1 lime leaf

1-inch/2.5-cm piece fresh ginger, sliced

¼ tsp chili paste, or to taste

7 oz/200 g large or medium raw shrimp, peeled and deveined

4–6 scallions, sliced

9 oz/250 g scallops

2 tbsp fresh cilantro leaves

salt

finely sliced red chiles, to garnish

Put the stock in a saucepan with the lemongrass, lime rind, ginger, and chili paste. Bring just to a boil, reduce the heat, cover, and simmer for 10–15 minutes.

Cut the shrimp almost in half lengthwise, keeping the tail intact.

Strain the stock, return to the saucepan, and bring to a simmer. Add the scallions and cook for 2–3 minutes. Taste and season with salt, if needed, and stir in a little more chili paste if desired.

Add the scallops and shrimp and poach for about 1 minute until they turn opaque and the shrimp curl.

Stir in the fresh cilantro leaves, ladle the soup into warmed bowls, dividing the shellfish evenly, and garnish with chiles.

Shrimp Laksa

serves 4

20–24 large raw unshelled shrimp

2 cups fish stock

pinch of salt

1 tsp peanut oil

2 cups coconut milk

2 tsp nam pla (Thai fish sauce)

½ tbsp lime juice

4 oz/115 g dried medium rice noodles

⅜ cup bean sprouts

sprigs of fresh cilantro, to garnish

for the laksa paste

6 fresh cilantro stalks with leaves

3 large garlic cloves, crushed

1 fresh red chile, seeded and chopped

1 lemongrass stalk, center part only, chopped

1-inch/2.5-cm piece fresh ginger, peeled and chopped

1½ tbsp shrimp paste

½ tsp ground turmeric

2 tbsp peanut oil

Buy unshelled shrimp, ideally with heads still intact, because you can add the shells and heads to the simmering stock to intensify the flavor.

Shell and devein the shrimp, and reserve. Put the fish stock, salt, and the shrimp heads, shells, and tails in a pan over high heat and slowly bring to a boil. Lower the heat and simmer for 10 minutes.

Meanwhile, make the laksa paste. Put all the ingredients except the oil in a food processor and blend. With the motor running, slowly add up to 2 tablespoons of oil just until a paste forms. (If your food processor is too large to work efficiently with this small quantity, use a mortar and pestle, or make double the quantity and keep leftovers tightly covered in the refrigerator to use another time.)

Heat the oil in a large pan over high heat. Add the paste and stir-fry until it is fragrant. Strain the stock through a strainer lined with cheesecloth. Stir the stock into the laksa paste, along with the coconut milk, nam pla, and lime juice. Bring to a boil, then lower the heat, cover, and simmer for 30 minutes.

Meanwhile, soak the noodles in a large bowl with enough lukewarm water to cover for 20 minutes, until soft. Alternatively, cook according to the package directions. Drain and set aside.

Add the shrimp and bean sprouts to the soup and continue simmering just until the shrimp turn opaque and curl. Divide the noodles among 4 bowls and ladle the soup over, making sure everyone gets an equal share of the shrimp. Garnish with the cilantro and serve.

Clam & Corn Chowder

serves 4

1 lb 10 oz/750 g clams, or 10 oz/280 g canned clams

2 tbsp dry white wine (if using fresh clams)

4 tsp butter

1 large onion, finely chopped

1 small carrot, finely diced

3 tbsp all-purpose flour

1¼ cups fish stock

¾ cup water (if using canned clams)

1 lb/450 g potatoes, diced

1 cup corn, thawed if frozen

2 cups whole milk

salt and pepper

chopped fresh parsley, to garnish

If using fresh clams, wash under cold running water. Discard any with broken shells or any that refuse to close when tapped. Put the clams into a heavy-bottom saucepan with the wine. Cover tightly, set over medium-high heat, and cook for 2–4 minutes, or until they open, shaking the pan occasionally. Discard any that remain closed. Remove the clams from the shells and strain the cooking liquid through a very fine mesh strainer; reserve both. If using canned clams, drain and rinse well.

Melt the butter in a large saucepan over medium-low heat. Add the onion and carrot and cook for 3–4 minutes, stirring frequently, until the onion is softened. Stir in the flour and continue cooking for 2 minutes.

Slowly add about half the stock and stir well, scraping the bottom of the pan to mix in the flour. Pour in the remaining stock and the reserved clam cooking liquid, or the water if using canned clams, and bring just to a boil, stirring.

Add the potatoes, corn, and milk and stir to combine. Reduce the heat and simmer gently, partially covered, for about 20 minutes, stirring occasionally, until all the vegetables are tender.

Chop the clams, if large. Stir in the clams and continue cooking for about 5 minutes until heated through. Taste and adjust the seasoning, if needed.

Ladle the soup into bowls and sprinkle with parsley.

Fennel & Tomato Soup with Shrimp

serves 4

- 2 tsp olive oil
- 1 large onion, halved and sliced
- 2 large fennel bulbs, halved and sliced
- 1 small potato, diced
- 3¾ cups water
- 1⅔ cups tomato juice, plus extra if needed
- 1 bay leaf
- 4½ oz/125 g cooked peeled small shrimp
- 2 tomatoes, skinned, seeded, and chopped
- ½ tsp snipped fresh dill
- salt and pepper
- dill sprigs or fennel fronds, to garnish

Heat the olive oil in a large saucepan over medium heat. Add the onion and fennel and cook for 3–4 minutes, stirring occasionally, until the onion is just softened.

Add the potato, water, tomato juice, and bay leaf with a large pinch of salt. Reduce the heat, cover, and simmer for about 25 minutes, stirring once or twice, until the vegetables are soft.

Allow the soup to cool slightly, then transfer to a food processor or blender and process until smooth, working in batches if necessary. (If using a food processor, strain off the cooking liquid and reserve. Purée the soup solids with enough cooking liquid to moisten them, then combine with the remaining liquid.)

Return the soup to the saucepan and add the shrimp. Simmer gently for about 10 minutes, to reheat the soup and allow it to absorb the shrimp flavor.

Stir in the tomatoes and dill. Taste and adjust the seasoning, adding salt, if needed, and pepper. Thin the soup with a little more tomato juice, if desired. Ladle into warmed bowls, garnish with dill or fennel fronds, and serve.

Genoese Fish Soup

serves 4

2 tbsp butter

1 onion, chopped

1 garlic clove, finely chopped

2 oz/55 g rindless bacon, diced

2 celery stalks, chopped

14 oz/400 g canned chopped tomatoes

$\frac{2}{3}$ cup dry white wine

$1\frac{1}{4}$ cups fish stock

4 fresh basil leaves, torn

2 tbsp chopped fresh flat-leaf parsley

1 lb/450 g whitefish fillets, such as cod or monkfish, skinned and chopped

4 oz/115 g cooked peeled shrimp

salt and pepper

Melt the butter in a large, heavy-bottom saucepan. Add the onion and garlic and cook over low heat, stirring occasionally, for 5 minutes, or until softened.

Add the bacon and celery and cook, stirring frequently, for an additional 2 minutes.

Add the tomatoes, wine, stock, basil, and 1 tablespoon of the parsley. Season to taste with salt and pepper. Bring to a boil, then reduce the heat and simmer for 10 minutes.

Add the fish and cook for 5 minutes, or until it is opaque. Add the shrimp and heat through gently for 3 minutes. Ladle into warmed serving bowls, garnish with the remaining chopped parsley, and serve immediately.

Cold Cucumber & Smoked Salmon Soup

serves 4

2 tsp oil

1 large onion, finely chopped

1 large cucumber, peeled, seeded, and sliced

1 small potato, diced

1 celery stalk, finely chopped

4 cups chicken or vegetable stock

1⅔ cups heavy cream

5½ oz/150 g smoked salmon, finely diced

2 tbsp snipped fresh chives

salt and pepper

Heat the oil in a large saucepan over medium heat. Add the onion and cook for about 3 minutes, until it begins to soften.

Add the cucumber, potato, celery, and stock, along with a large pinch of salt, if using unsalted stock. Bring to a boil, reduce the heat, cover, and cook gently for about 20 minutes until the vegetables are tender.

Allow the soup to cool slightly, then transfer to a food processor or blender, working in batches if necessary. Purée the soup until smooth. (If using a food processor, strain off the cooking liquid and reserve it. Purée the soup solids with enough cooking liquid to moisten them, then combine with the remaining liquid.)

Transfer the puréed soup into a large container. Cover and refrigerate until cold.

Stir the cream, salmon, and chives into the soup. If time permits, chill for at least 1 hour to allow the flavors to blend. Taste and adjust the seasoning, adding salt, if needed, and pepper. Ladle into chilled bowls and serve.

Seafood Chowder

serves 4

- 2 lb 4 oz/1 kg live mussels
- 4 tbsp all-purpose flour
- 6¼ cups fish stock
- 1 tbsp butter
- 1 large onion, finely chopped
- 12 oz/350 g skinless whitefish fillets, such as cod or sole
- 7 oz/200 g cooked or raw shrimp, peeled and deveined
- 1¼ cups heavy cream
- salt and pepper
- snipped fresh dill, to garnish

Soak the mussels in lightly salted water for 10 minutes. Scrub the shells under cold running water and pull off any beards. Discard any mussels with broken shells or any that refuse to close when tapped. Put the rest in a large heavy-bottom saucepan with a little water, bring to the boil and cook over a high heat for 4 minutes, or until the mussels open. Remove from the heat and discard any that remain closed. When they are cool enough to handle, remove the mussels from the shells, adding any additional juices to the cooking liquid. Strain the cooking liquid through a cheesecloth-lined strainer and reserve.

Put the flour in a mixing bowl and very slowly whisk in enough of the stock to make a thick paste. Whisk in a little more stock to make a smooth liquid.

Melt the butter in a heavy-bottom saucepan over medium-low heat. Add the onion, cover, and cook for about 5 minutes, stirring frequently, until it softens.

Add the remaining fish stock and bring to a boil. Slowly whisk in the flour mixture until well combined and bring back to a boil, whisking constantly. Add the mussel cooking liquid. Season with salt, if needed, and pepper. Reduce the heat and simmer, partially covered, for 15 minutes.

Add the fish and mussels and continue simmering, stirring occasionally, for about 5 minutes, or until the fish is cooked and begins to flake.

Stir in the shrimp and cream. Taste and adjust the seasoning. Simmer for a few minutes longer to heat through. Ladle into warmed bowls, sprinkle with dill, and serve.

Seared Scallops in Garlic Broth

serves 4

1 large garlic bulb (about 3½ oz/ 100 g), separated into unpeeled cloves

1 celery stalk, chopped

1 carrot, chopped

1 onion, chopped

10 peppercorns

5–6 parsley stems

5 cups water

8 oz/225 g large sea scallops

1 tbsp oil

salt and pepper

fresh cilantro leaves, to garnish

Combine the garlic cloves, celery, carrot, onion, peppercorns, parsley stems, and water in a saucepan with a good pinch of salt. Bring to a boil, reduce the heat, and simmer, partially covered, for 30–45 minutes.

Strain the stock into a clean saucepan. Taste and adjust the seasoning, and keep hot.

If using sea scallops, slice in half to form 2 thinner rounds from each. (If the scallops are very large, slice them into 3 rounds.) Sprinkle with salt and pepper.

Heat the oil in a skillet over medium-high heat and cook the scallops on one side for 1–2 minutes, until lightly browned and the flesh becomes opaque.

Divide the scallops among 4 warmed shallow bowls, arranging them browned-side up. Ladle the soup over the scallops, then float a few cilantro leaves on top. Serve immediately.

Squid, Chorizo & Tomato Soup

serves 6

1 lb/450 g cleaned squid

5½ oz/150 g lean chorizo, peeled and very finely diced

1 onion, finely chopped

1 celery stalk, thinly sliced

1 carrot, thinly sliced

2 garlic cloves, finely chopped or crushed

14 oz/400 g canned chopped tomatoes

5 cups fish stock

½ tsp ground cumin

pinch of saffron

1 bay leaf

chili paste (optional)

salt and pepper

fresh chopped parsley, to garnish

Cut off the squid tentacles and cut into bite-sized pieces. Slice the bodies into rings.

Place a large saucepan over medium-low heat and add the chorizo. Cook for 5–10 minutes, stirring frequently, until it renders most of its fat. Remove with a slotted spoon and drain on paper towels.

Pour off all the fat from the pan and add the onion, celery, carrot, and garlic. Cover and cook for 3–4 minutes, until the onion is slightly softened.

Stir in the tomatoes, fish stock, cumin, saffron, bay leaf, and chorizo.

Add the squid to the soup. Bring almost to a boil, reduce the heat, cover, and cook gently for 40–45 minutes, or until the squid and carrot are tender, stirring occasionally.

Taste the soup and stir in a little chili paste, if using, for a spicier flavour. Season with salt and pepper. Ladle into warmed bowls, sprinkle with parsley, and serve.

Lobster Bisque

serves 4

1 lb/450 g cooked lobster
3 tbsp butter
1 small carrot, grated
1 celery stalk, finely chopped
1 leek, finely chopped
1 small onion, finely chopped
2 shallots, finely chopped
3 tbsp brandy or Cognac
1/4 cup dry white wine
5 cups water
1 tbsp tomato paste
1/2 cup heavy cream, or to taste
6 tbsp all-purpose flour
2–3 tbsp water
salt and pepper
snipped fresh chives, to garnish

Pull off the lobster tail. With the legs up, cut the body in half lengthwise. Scoop out the tomalley (the soft pale greenish-gray part) and, if it is a female, the roe (the solid red-orange part). Reserve these together, covered and refrigerated. Remove the meat and cut into bite-sized pieces; cover and refrigerate. Chop the shell into large pieces.

Melt half the butter in a large saucepan over medium heat and add the lobster shell pieces. Cook until brown bits begin to stick on the bottom of the pan. Add the carrot, celery, leek, onion, and shallots. Cook, stirring, for 1½–2 minutes (do not let it burn). Add the brandy and wine and bubble for 1 minute. Pour over the water, add the tomato paste and a large pinch of salt, and bring to a boil. Reduce the heat, simmer for 30 minutes, and strain the stock, discarding the solids.

Melt the remaining butter in a small saucepan and add the tomalley and roe, if any. Add the cream, whisk to mix well, remove from the heat, and set aside.

Put the flour in a small mixing bowl and very slowly whisk in the cold water. Stir in a little of the hot stock mixture to make a smooth liquid.

Bring the remaining lobster stock to the boil and whisk in the flour mixture. Boil gently for 4–5 minutes, or until the soup thickens. Press the tomalley, roe and cream mixture through a strainer into the soup. Simmer until heated through.

Taste the soup and adjust the seasoning, adding more cream if desired. Ladle into warmed bowls, sprinkle with chives, and serve.

Tuna Chowder

serves 4

2 tbsp butter

1 large garlic clove, chopped

1 large onion, sliced

1 carrot, peeled and chopped

2½ cups fish stock

14 oz/400 g potatoes, peeled and cut into bite-size chunks

14 oz/400 g canned chopped tomatoes

14 oz/400 g canned cannellini beans, drained

1 tbsp tomato paste

1 zucchini, trimmed and chopped

8 oz/225 g canned tuna in brine, drained

1 tbsp chopped fresh basil

1 tbsp chopped fresh parsley

scant ½ cup heavy cream

salt and pepper

sprigs of fresh basil, to garnish

Melt the butter in a large pan over low heat. Add the garlic and onion and cook, stirring, for 3 minutes, until slightly softened. Add the carrot and cook for another 5 minutes, stirring. Pour in the stock, then add the potatoes, tomatoes, beans, and tomato paste. Season with salt and pepper. Bring to a boil, then reduce the heat, cover the pan, and simmer for 20 minutes.

Add the zucchini, tuna, and chopped basil and parsley and cook for another 15 minutes. Stir in the cream and cook the soup very gently for another 2 minutes.

Remove from the heat and ladle into serving bowls. Garnish with sprigs of fresh basil, and serve.

Creamy Oyster Soup

serves 4

12 oysters

2 tbsp butter

2 shallots, finely chopped

5 tbsp white wine

1¼ cups fish stock

¾ cup heavy cream

2 tbsp cornstarch, dissolved in 2 tbsp cold water

salt and pepper

caviar or lumpfish roe, to garnish (optional)

To open the oysters, hold flat-side up, over a strainer set over a bowl to catch the juices, and push an oyster knife into the hinge. Work it around until you can pry off the top shell. When all the oysters have been opened, strain the liquid through a strainer lined with damp cheesecloth. Remove any bits of shell stuck to the oysters and reserve them in their liquid.

Melt half the butter in a saucepan over low heat. Add the shallots and cook gently for about 5 minutes, until just softened, stirring frequently; do not allow them to brown.

Add the wine, bring to a boil, and boil for 1 minute. Stir in the fish stock, bring back to a boil, and boil for 3–4 minutes. Reduce the heat to a gentle simmer.

Add the oysters and their liquid and poach for about 1 minute, until they become more firm but are still tender. Remove the oysters with a slotted spoon and reserve, covered. Strain the stock.

Bring the strained stock to a boil in a clean saucepan. Add the cream and bring back to a boil.

Stir the dissolved cornstarch into the soup and boil gently for 2–3 minutes, stirring frequently, until slightly thickened. Add the oysters and cook for 1–2 minutes to reheat them. Taste and adjust the seasoning, if necessary, and ladle the soup into warmed bowls. Top each serving with a teaspoon of caviar or roe, if using.

Mixed Fish Soup

serves 4

1 tbsp butter

2 shallots, chopped

1 leek, trimmed and sliced

3 tbsp all-purpose flour

generous 2 cups fish stock

1 bay leaf

generous 2 cups milk

2 tbsp dry sherry

2 tbsp lemon juice

10½ oz/300 g haddock fillets, skinned

10½ oz/300 g cod fillets, skinned

7 oz/200 g canned or freshly cooked crabmeat

5½ oz/150 g canned corn kernels, drained

generous ¾ cup heavy cream

salt and pepper

sprigs of fresh dill and wedges of lemon, to garnish

Melt the butter in a large pan over medium heat. Add the shallots and leek and cook, stirring, for about 3 minutes, until slightly softened. In a bowl, mix the flour with enough stock to make a smooth paste, then stir it into the pan. Cook, stirring, for 2 minutes, then gradually stir in the remaining stock. Add the bay leaf and season with salt and pepper. Bring to a boil, then lower the heat. Pour in the milk and sherry and stir in the lemon juice. Simmer for 15 minutes.

Rinse the haddock and cod under cold running water, then drain and cut into bite-size chunks. Add to the soup with the crabmeat and corn. Cook for 15 minutes, until the fish is tender and cooked through. Stir in the cream. Cook for another 2–3 minutes, then remove from the heat and discard the bay leaf.

Ladle into serving bowls, garnish with sprigs of fresh dill and lemon wedges, and serve.

Crab & Vegetable Soup

serves 4

2 tbsp chili oil

1 garlic clove, chopped

4 scallions, trimmed and sliced

2 red bell peppers, seeded and chopped

1 tbsp grated fresh ginger

4 cups fish stock

scant ½ cup coconut milk

scant ½ cup rice wine or sherry

2 tbsp lime juice

1 tbsp grated lime zest

6 kaffir lime leaves, finely shredded

10½ oz/300 g freshly cooked crabmeat

7 oz/200 g freshly cooked crab claws

5½ oz/150 g canned corn kernels, drained

1 tbsp of chopped cilantro, plus a few sprigs to garnish

salt and pepper

Heat the oil in a large pan over medium heat. Add the garlic and scallions and cook, stirring, for about 3 minutes, until slightly softened. Add the bell peppers and ginger and cook for another 4 minutes, stirring. Pour in the stock and season with salt and pepper. Bring to a boil, then lower the heat. Pour in the coconut milk, rice wine, and lime juice and stir in the grated lime zest and kaffir lime leaves. Simmer for 15 minutes.

Add the crabmeat and crab claws to the soup with the corn and cilantro. Cook the soup for 15 minutes, until the fish is tender and cooked right through.

Remove from the heat and ladle into serving bowls. Garnish with fresh cilantro and serve.

Shrimp & Vegetable Bisque

serves 4

3 tbsp butter

1 garlic clove, chopped

1 onion, sliced

1 carrot, peeled and chopped

1 celery stalk, trimmed and sliced

5 cups fish stock

4 tbsp red wine

1 tbsp tomato paste

1 bay leaf

1 lb 5 oz/600 g shrimp, peeled and deveined

scant ½ cup heavy cream

salt and pepper

swirls of single cream and whole cooked shrimp, to garnish

Melt the butter in a large pan over medium heat. Add the garlic and onion and cook, stirring, for 3 minutes, until slightly softened. Add the carrot and celery and cook for another 3 minutes, stirring. Pour in the stock and red wine, then add the tomato paste and bay leaf. Season with salt and pepper. Bring to a boil, then lower the heat and simmer for 20 minutes. Remove from the heat and let cool for 10 minutes, then remove and discard the bay leaf.

Transfer half of the soup into a food processor and blend until smooth (you may need to do this in batches). Return to the pan with the rest of the soup. Add the shrimp and cook the soup over low heat for 5–6 minutes.

Stir in the cream and cook for another 2 minutes, then remove from the heat and ladle into serving bowls. Garnish with swirls of light cream and whole cooked shrimp, and serve at once.

Fish Chowder

serves 4

- 1 tbsp butter
- 1 onion, chopped
- 3 tbsp all-purpose flour
- generous 2 cups fish stock
- 1 bay leaf
- salt and pepper
- generous 2 cups milk
- 2 tbsp dry white wine
- juice and grated rind of 1 lemon
- 1 lb/450 g haddock fillets, skinned
- 4½ oz/125 g frozen corn kernels, thawed
- 9 oz/250 g shrimp, cooked and peeled
- generous ¾ cup heavy cream
- whole cooked shrimp, to garnish
- fresh green salad, to serve

Melt the butter in a large pan over medium heat. Add the onion and cook, stirring, for about 3 minutes, until slightly softened. In a bowl, mix the flour with enough stock to make a smooth paste and stir it into the pan. Cook, stirring, for 2 minutes, then gradually stir in the remaining stock. Add the bay leaf and season with salt and pepper. Bring to a boil, then lower the heat. Pour in the milk and wine, and stir in the lemon juice and grated rind. Simmer for 15 minutes.

Rinse the haddock under cold running water, then drain, and cut into bite-size chunks. Add them to the soup with the corn. Cook for 15 minutes, until the fish is tender and cooked through. Stir in the shrimp and the cream. Cook for another 2–3 minutes, then remove from the heat and discard the bay leaf.

Ladle into serving bowls, garnish with whole cooked shrimp, and serve with a fresh green salad.

3

Meat

Beef & Vegetable Soup

serves 4

1/3 cup pearl barley, rinsed and drained

5 cups beef stock

1 tsp dried mixed herbs

8 oz/225 g lean sirloin or porterhouse steak

1 large carrot, diced

1 leek, shredded

1 medium onion, chopped

2 celery stalks, sliced

salt and pepper

2 tbsp chopped fresh parsley, to garnish

Place the pearl barley in a large saucepan. Pour over the stock and add the mixed herbs. Bring to a boil, cover, and simmer gently over low heat for 10 minutes.

Meanwhile, trim any fat from the beef and cut the meat into thin strips.

Skim away any foam that has risen to the top of the stock with a flat ladle.

Add the beef, carrot, leek, onion, and celery to the pan. Bring back to a boil, cover, and simmer for about 1 hour or until the pearl barley, beef, and vegetables are just tender.

Skim away any remaining foam that has risen to the top of the soup with a flat ladle. Blot the surface with absorbent paper towels to remove any fat. Adjust the seasoning according to taste.

Ladle the soup into warmed bowls, garnish with chopped parsley, and serve hot.

EASTER SEALS 2017

Spicy Beef & Noodle Soup

serves 4

4 cups beef stock

2/3 cup vegetable or peanut oil

3 oz/85 g rice vermicelli noodles

2 shallots, thinly sliced

2 garlic cloves, crushed

1-inch/2.5-cm piece fresh ginger, thinly sliced

8 oz/225 g piece beef tenderloin, cut into thin strips

2 tbsp Thai green curry paste

2 tbsp Thai soy sauce

1 tbsp fish sauce

chopped fresh cilantro, to garnish

Pour the stock into a large pan and bring to a boil. Meanwhile, heat the oil in a wok or large skillet. Add a third of the noodles and cook for 10–20 seconds, until they have puffed up. Lift out with tongs, drain on paper towels, and set aside. Discard all but 2 tablespoons of the oil.

Add the shallots, garlic, and ginger to the wok or skillet and stir-fry for 1 minute. Add the beef and curry paste and stir-fry for an additional 3–4 minutes, until tender.

Add the beef mixture, the uncooked noodles, soy sauce, and fish sauce to the pan of stock and simmer for 2–3 minutes, until the noodles have swelled. Serve hot, garnished with the chopped cilantro and the reserved crispy noodles.

Beef & Bean Soup

serves 4

2 tbsp vegetable oil

1 large onion, finely chopped

2 garlic cloves, finely chopped

1 green bell pepper, seeded and sliced

2 carrots, sliced

14 oz/400 g canned black-eyed peas

1 cup fresh ground beef

1 tsp each ground cumin, chili powder, and paprika

1/4 head of cabbage, sliced

8 oz/225 g tomatoes, peeled and chopped

2 1/2 cups beef stock

salt and pepper

Heat the oil in a large pan over medium heat. Add the onion and garlic and cook, stirring frequently, for 5 minutes, or until softened. Add the bell pepper and carrots and cook for an additional 5 minutes.

Meanwhile, drain the peas, reserving the liquid from the can. Place two thirds of the peas, reserving the remainder, in a food processor or blender with the pea liquid and process until smooth.

Add the ground beef to the pan and cook, stirring constantly to break up any lumps, until well browned. Add the spices and cook, stirring, for 2 minutes. Add the cabbage, tomatoes, stock, and puréed peas and season to taste with salt and pepper. Bring to a boil, then reduce the heat, cover, and let simmer for 15 minutes, or until the vegetables are tender.

Stir in the reserved peas, cover, and simmer for an additional 5 minutes. Ladle the soup into warmed soup bowls and serve.

Beef Consommé with Eggs & Parmesan

serves 4

6⅓ cups beef consommé or beef stock

3 eggs

½ cup fresh white breadcrumbs

½ cup Parmesan cheese, freshly grated

salt

Pour the consommé or stock into a pan and heat gently, stirring occasionally.

Meanwhile, beat the eggs in a bowl until combined, then stir in the breadcrumbs and Parmesan. Season with salt.

As soon as the consommé or stock comes to a boil, add the egg mixture. When it floats to the surface, stir with a fork to break it up. Ladle into warmed soup bowls and then serve immediately.

Mexican-Style Beef & Rice Soup

serves 4

3 tbsp olive oil

1 lb 2 oz/500 g boneless braising beef, cut into 1-inch/2.5-cm pieces

2/3 cup red wine

1 onion, finely chopped

1 green bell pepper, seeded and finely chopped

1 small fresh red chile, seeded and finely chopped

2 garlic cloves, finely chopped

1 carrot, finely chopped

1/4 tsp ground cilantro

1/4 tsp ground cumin

1/8 tsp ground cinnamon

1/4 tsp dried oregano

1 bay leaf

grated rind of 1/2 orange

14 oz/400 g canned chopped tomatoes

5 cups beef stock

1/4 cup long-grain white rice

3 tbsp raisins

1/2 oz/15 g semisweet chocolate, melted

Heat half the oil in a large skillet over medium-high heat. Add the meat in one layer and cook until well browned, turning to color all sides. Remove the pan from the heat and pour in the wine.

Heat the remaining oil in a large saucepan over medium heat. Add the onion, cover, and cook for about 3 minutes, stirring occasionally, until just softened. Add the green bell pepper, chile, garlic, and carrot and continue cooking, covered, for 3 minutes.

Add the cilantro, cumin, cinnamon, oregano, bay leaf, and orange rind. Stir in the tomatoes and stock, along with the beef and wine. Bring almost to a boil and when the mixture begins to bubble, reduce the heat to low. Cover and simmer gently, stirring occasionally, for about 1 hour until the meat is tender.

Stir in the rice, raisins, and chocolate, and continue cooking, stirring occasionally, for about 30 minutes until the rice is tender.

Ladle into warmed bowls and serve.

Beef Broth with Herbs & Vegetables

serves 4–6

7 oz/200 g celeriac, peeled and finely diced

2 large carrots, finely diced

2 tsp chopped fresh marjoram leaves

2 tsp chopped fresh parsley

2 plum tomatoes, skinned, seeded, and diced

salt and pepper

for the beef stock

1 lb 4 oz/550g boneless beef shin or braising beef, cut into large cubes

1 lb 10 oz/750 g veal, beef, or pork bones

2 onions, quartered

10 cups water

4 garlic cloves, sliced

2 carrots, sliced

1 large leek, sliced

1 celery stalk, cut into 2-inch/5-cm pieces

1 bay leaf

4–5 sprigs of fresh thyme, or 1/4 tsp dried thyme

salt

Preheat the oven to 375°F/190°C. To make the stock, trim as much fat as possible from the beef and put in a large roasting pan with the bones and onions. Roast for 30–40 minutes, turning once or twice. Transfer to a large flameproof casserole and discard the fat.

Add the water and bring to a boil. Skim off any foam that rises to the surface. Reduce the heat and add the garlic, carrots, leek, celery, bay leaf, thyme, and salt. Simmer very gently, uncovered, for 4 hours. Do not stir. If the ingredients emerge from the liquid, top up with water.

Gently ladle the stock through a cheesecloth-lined strainer into a large container and remove as much fat as possible. Save the meat for another purpose, if desired, and discard the bones and vegetables. (There should be about 8 cups of stock.)

Boil the stock very gently until it is reduced to 6 1/4 cups, or if the stock already has concentrated flavor, measure out that amount and save the rest for another purpose. Taste the stock and adjust the seasoning if necessary.

Bring a saucepan of salted water to a boil and drop in the celeriac and carrots. Reduce the heat, cover, and boil gently for about 15 minutes until tender. Drain.

Add the marjoram and parsley to the boiling beef stock. Divide the cooked vegetables and diced tomatoes among warmed bowls, ladle over the boiling stock, and serve.

Chunky Potato & Beef Soup

serves 4

2 tbsp vegetable oil

8 oz/225 g lean braising steak, cut into strips

8 oz/225 g new potatoes, halved

1 carrot, diced

2 celery stalks, sliced

2 leeks, sliced

3½ cups beef stock

8 baby corn, sliced

1 bouquet garni

2 tbsp dry sherry

salt and pepper

chopped fresh parsley, to garnish

Heat the vegetable oil in a large pan. Add the strips of meat to the pan and cook for 3 minutes, turning constantly. Add the potatoes, carrot, celery, and leeks to the pan. Cook for an additional 5 minutes, stirring.

Pour the beef stock into the pan and bring to a boil. Reduce the heat until the liquid is simmering, then add the baby corn and the bouquet garni. Cook for an additional 20 minutes, or until cooked through.

Remove and discard the bouquet garni. Stir the dry sherry into the soup, then season to taste with salt and pepper.

Ladle the soup into warmed bowls, garnish with chopped parsley and serve.

Asian Lamb Soup

serves 4

5½ oz/150 g lean tender lamb, such as neck fillet or leg steak

2 garlic cloves, very finely chopped

2 tbsp soy sauce

5 cups chicken stock

1 tbsp grated fresh ginger

2-inch/5-cm piece lemongrass, sliced into very thin rounds

¼ tsp chili paste, or to taste

6–8 cherry tomatoes, quartered

4 scallions, thinly sliced

1¾ oz/50 g bean sprouts, snapped in half

2 tbsp cilantro leaves

1 tsp olive oil

Trim all visible fat from the lamb and slice the meat thinly. Cut the slices into bite-sized pieces. Spread the meat in one layer on a plate and sprinkle over the garlic and 1 tablespoon of the soy sauce. Leave to marinate, covered, for at least 10 minutes or up to 1 hour.

Put the stock in a saucepan with the ginger, lemongrass, remaining soy sauce, and the chili paste. Bring just to a boil, reduce the heat, cover, and simmer for 10–15 minutes.

When ready to serve the soup, drop the tomatoes, scallions, bean sprouts, and cilantro leaves into the stock.

Heat the oil in a skillet and add the lamb with its marinade. Stir-fry the lamb just until it is no longer red and divide among the warmed bowls.

Ladle over the hot stock and serve immediately.

Hearty Broth

serves 4

1 tbsp vegetable oil

1 lb 2 oz/500 g lean neck of lamb

1 large onion, sliced

2 carrots, sliced

2 leeks, sliced

4 cups vegetable stock

1 bay leaf

sprigs of fresh parsley

2 oz/55 g pearl barley, rinsed and drained

salt and pepper

Heat the vegetable oil in a large, heavy-bottom saucepan and add the pieces of lamb, turning them to seal and brown on both sides. Lift the lamb out of the pan and set aside until ready to use.

Add the onion, carrots, and leeks to the saucepan and cook gently for about 3 minutes.

Return the lamb to the saucepan and add the vegetable stock, bay leaf, parsley, and pearl barley to the saucepan. Bring the mixture in the pan to a boil, then reduce the heat. Cover and simmer for 1½ –2 hours.

Discard the parsley sprigs. Lift the pieces of lamb from the broth and allow them to cool slightly. Remove the bones and any fat and chop the meat. Return the lamb to the broth and reheat gently. Season to taste with salt and pepper.

It is advisable to prepare this soup a day ahead, then leave it to cool, cover, and refrigerate overnight. When ready to serve, remove and discard the layer of fat from the surface and reheat the soup gently. Ladle into warmed bowls and serve immediately.

Spicy Lamb Soup with Chickpeas & Zucchini

serves 4–6

1–2 tbsp olive oil

1 lb/450 g lean boneless lamb, trimmed of fat and cut into ½-inch/1-cm cubes

1 onion, finely chopped

2–3 garlic cloves, crushed

5 cups water

14 oz/400 g canned chopped tomatoes

1 bay leaf

½ tsp each of dried thyme and oregano

⅛ tsp ground cinnamon

¼ tsp each of ground cumin and turmeric

1 tsp harissa

14 oz/400 g canned chickpeas, rinsed and drained

1 each of carrot, potato and zucchini, diced

3½ oz/100 g fresh peas

fresh mint sprigs, to garnish

Heat 1 tablespoon of the oil in a large saucepan or cast-iron casserole over medium-high heat. Add the lamb, in batches if necessary to avoid crowding the pan, and cook until evenly browned on all sides, adding a little more oil if needed. Remove the meat with a slotted spoon when browned.

Reduce the heat and add the onion and garlic to the pan. Cook, stirring frequently, for 1–2 minutes.

Add the water and return all the meat to the pan. Bring just to a boil and skim off any foam that rises to the surface. Reduce the heat and stir in the tomatoes, bay leaf, thyme, oregano, cinnamon, cumin, turmeric, and harissa. Simmer for about 1 hour, or until the meat is very tender. Discard the bay leaf.

Stir in the chickpeas, carrot, and potato and simmer for 15 minutes. Add the zucchini and peas and continue simmering for 15–20 minutes, or until all the vegetables are tender.

Ladle the soup into warmed bowls and garnish with mint.

Lamb & Rice Soup

serves 4

- 5½ oz/150 g lean lamb
- scant ¼ cup rice
- 3½ cups lamb stock
- 1 leek, sliced
- 1 garlic clove, thinly sliced
- 2 tsp light soy sauce
- 1 tsp rice wine vinegar
- 1 medium open-cap mushroom, thinly sliced
- salt

Using a sharp knife, trim any visible fat from the lamb and cut the meat into thin strips. Set aside until required.

Bring a large pan of lightly salted water to a boil and add the rice. Return to a boil, stir once, reduce the heat, and cook for 10–15 minutes, or until tender. Drain the cooked rice, rinse under cold running water, drain again, and set aside.

Place the lamb stock in a large pan and bring to a boil. Add the lamb strips, leek, garlic, soy sauce, and rice wine vinegar, reduce the heat, cover, and let simmer for 10 minutes, or until the lamb is tender and cooked through.

Add the mushroom slices and cooked rice to the pan and cook for an additional 2–3 minutes, or until the mushrooms are completely cooked through.

Ladle the soup into warmed bowls and serve immediately.

Split Pea & Ham Soup

serves 6–8

- 1 lb 2 oz/500 g split green peas
- 1 tbsp olive oil
- 1 large onion, finely chopped
- 1 large carrot, finely chopped
- 1 celery stalk, finely chopped
- 4 cups chicken or vegetable stock
- 4 cups water
- 8 oz/225 g lean smoked ham, finely diced
- ¼ tsp dried thyme
- ¼ tsp dried marjoram
- 1 bay leaf
- salt and pepper

Rinse the peas under cold running water. Put in a saucepan and cover generously with water. Bring to a boil and boil for 3 minutes, skimming off the foam from the surface. Drain the peas.

Heat the oil in a large saucepan over medium heat. Add the onion and cook for 3–4 minutes, stirring occasionally, until just softened.

Add the carrot and celery and continue cooking for 2 minutes. Add the peas, pour over the stock and water, and stir to combine.

Bring just to a boil and stir the ham into the soup. Add the thyme, marjoram, and bay leaf. Reduce the heat, cover, and cook gently for 1–1½ hours, until the ingredients are very soft. Remove the bay leaf.

Taste and adjust the seasoning, adding salt and pepper to taste. Ladle into warmed soup bowls and serve.

Cheese & Bacon Soup

serves 4

2 tbsp butter

2 garlic cloves, chopped

1 large onion, sliced

9 oz/250 g smoked lean bacon, chopped

2 large leeks, trimmed and sliced

2 tbsp all-purpose flour

4 cups vegetable stock

1 lb/450 g potatoes, chopped

scant ½ cup heavy cream

3 cups grated cheddar cheese, plus extra to garnish

salt and pepper

Melt the butter in a large pan over medium heat. Add the garlic and onion and cook, stirring, for 3 minutes, until slightly softened. Add the chopped bacon and leeks and cook for another 3 minutes, stirring.

In a bowl, mix the flour with enough stock to make a smooth paste and stir it into the pan. Cook, stirring, for 2 minutes. Pour in the remaining stock, then add the potatoes. Season with salt and pepper. Bring the soup to a boil, then lower the heat and simmer gently for 25 minutes, until the potatoes are tender and cooked through.

Stir in the cream and cook for 5 minutes, then gradually stir in the cheese until melted. Remove from the heat and ladle into individual serving bowls. Garnish with grated cheddar cheese and serve immediately.

Sausage & Red Cabbage Soup

serves 4

2 tbsp olive oil
1 garlic clove, chopped
1 large onion, chopped
1 large leek, sliced
2 tbsp cornstarch
4 cups vegetable stock
1 lb/450 g potatoes, sliced
7 oz/200 g skinless sausages, sliced
5½ oz/150 g red cabbage, chopped
7 oz/200 g canned black-eyed peas, drained
½ cup heavy cream
salt and pepper
ground paprika, to garnish

Heat the oil in a large pan. Add the garlic and onion and cook over medium heat, stirring, for 3 minutes, until slightly softened. Add the leek and cook for another 3 minutes, stirring.

In a bowl, mix the cornstarch with enough stock to make a smooth paste, then stir it into the pan. Cook, stirring, for 2 minutes. Stir in the remaining stock, then add the potatoes and sausages. Season with salt and pepper. Bring to a boil, then lower the heat and simmer for 25 minutes.

Add the red cabbage and black-eyed peas and cook for 10 minutes, then stir in the cream and cook for another 5 minutes. Remove from the heat and ladle into serving bowls. Garnish with ground paprika and serve immediately.

Pork & Vegetable Broth

serves 4

- 1 tbsp chili oil
- 1 garlic clove, chopped
- 3 scallions, sliced
- 1 red bell pepper, seeded and finely sliced
- 2 tbsp cornstarch
- 4 cups vegetable stock
- 1 tbsp soy sauce
- 2 tbsp rice wine or dry sherry
- 5½ oz/150 g pork tenderloin, sliced
- 1 tbsp finely chopped lemongrass
- 1 small red chile, seeded and finely chopped
- 1 tbsp grated fresh ginger
- 4 oz/115 g fine egg noodles
- 7 oz/200 g canned water chestnuts, drained and sliced
- salt and pepper

Heat the oil in a large pan. Add the garlic and scallions and cook over medium heat, stirring, for 3 minutes, until slightly softened. Add the bell pepper and cook for an additional 5 minutes, stirring.

In a bowl, mix the cornstarch with enough of the stock to make a smooth paste and stir it into the pan. Cook, stirring, for 2 minutes. Stir in the remaining stock and the soy sauce and rice wine, then add the pork, lemongrass, chile, and ginger. Season with salt and pepper. Bring to a boil, then lower the heat and simmer for 25 minutes.

Bring a separate pan of water to a boil, add the noodles, and cook for 3 minutes. Remove from the heat, drain, then add the noodles to the soup along with the water chestnuts. Cook for another 2 minutes, then remove from the heat and ladle into warmed bowls.

Pork Chili Soup

serves 4

2 tsp olive oil

1 lb 2 oz/500 g fresh lean ground pork

1 onion, finely chopped

1 celery stalk, finely chopped

1 red bell pepper, cored, seeded, and finely chopped

2–3 garlic cloves, finely chopped

3 tbsp tomato paste

14 oz/400 g canned chopped tomatoes

2 cups chicken or meat stock

1/8 tsp ground cilantro

1/8 tsp ground cumin

1/4 tsp dried oregano

1 tsp mild chili powder, or to taste

salt and pepper

sour cream, to serve

Heat the oil in a large saucepan over medium-high heat. Add the pork, season with salt and pepper, and cook until no longer pink, stirring frequently. Reduce the heat to medium and add the onion, celery, red bell pepper, and garlic. Cover and continue cooking for 5 minutes, stirring occasionally, until the onion is softened.

Add the tomato paste, tomatoes, and the stock. Add the cilantro, cumin, oregano, and chili powder. Stir the ingredients in to combine well.

Bring just to a boil, reduce the heat to low, cover, and simmer for 30–40 minutes until all the vegetables are very tender. Taste and adjust the seasoning, adding more chili powder if you like it hotter.

Ladle the soup into warmed bowls and serve with a spoonful of soured cream.

Chorizo & Red Kidney Bean Soup

serves 4

2 tbsp olive oil

2 garlic cloves, chopped

2 red onions, chopped

1 red bell pepper, seeded and chopped

2 tbsp cornstarch

4 cups vegetable stock

1 lb/450 g potatoes, peeled, halved, and sliced

5½ oz/150 g chorizo, sliced

2 zucchini, trimmed and sliced

7 oz/200 g canned red kidney beans, drained

½ cup heavy cream

salt and pepper

Heat the oil in a large pan. Add the garlic and onions and cook over medium heat, stirring, for 3 minutes, until slightly softened. Add the bell pepper and cook for another 3 minutes, stirring. In a bowl, mix the cornstarch with enough stock to make a smooth paste and stir it into the pan. Cook, stirring, for 2 minutes. Stir in the remaining stock, then add the potatoes and season with salt and pepper. Bring to a boil, then lower the heat and simmer for 25 minutes, until the vegetables are tender.

Add the chorizo, zucchini, and kidney beans to the pan. Cook for 10 minutes, then stir in the cream and cook for another 5 minutes. Remove from the heat and ladle into serving bowls.

Bacon & Lentil Soup

serves 4

1 lb/450 g thick, rindless smoked bacon strips, diced

1 onion, chopped

2 carrots, sliced

2 celery stalks, chopped

1 turnip, chopped

1 large potato, chopped

generous 2¼ cups Puy lentils

1 bouquet garni

4 cups water or chicken stock

salt and pepper

Heat a large, heavy-bottomed pan or flameproof casserole. Add the bacon and cook over medium heat, stirring, for 4–5 minutes, or until the fat runs. Add the chopped onion, carrots, celery, turnip, and potato and cook, stirring frequently, for 5 minutes.

Add the lentils and bouquet garni and pour in the water. Bring to a boil, reduce the heat, and simmer for 1 hour, or until the lentils are tender.

Remove and discard the bouquet garni and season the soup to taste with pepper, and with salt if necessary. Remove from the heat, ladle into warmed bowls and serve.

4

Chicken & Poultry

Cream of Chicken Soup

serves 4

3 tbsp butter

4 shallots, chopped

1 leek, sliced

1 lb/450 g skinless chicken breasts, chopped

2½ cups chicken stock

1 tbsp chopped fresh parsley

1 tbsp chopped fresh thyme, plus extra sprigs to garnish

¾ cup heavy cream

salt and pepper

Melt the butter in a large pan over medium heat. Add the shallots and cook, stirring, for 3 minutes, until slightly softened. Add the leek and cook for another 5 minutes, stirring. Add the chicken, stock, and herbs, and season with salt and pepper. Bring to a boil, then lower the heat and simmer for 25 minutes, until the chicken is tender and cooked through. Remove from the heat and let cool for 10 minutes.

Transfer the soup into a food processor or blender and process until smooth (you may need to do this in batches). Return the soup to the rinsed-out pan and warm over low heat for 5 minutes.

Stir in the cream and cook for another 2 minutes, then remove from the heat and ladle into serving bowls. Garnish with sprigs of thyme and serve immediately.

Chicken, Rice & Vegetable Soup

serves 4

6¼ cups chicken stock

2 small carrots, very thinly sliced

1 celery stalk, finely diced

1 baby leek, halved lengthwise and thinly sliced

4 oz/115 g petit pois, defrosted if frozen

1 cup cooked rice

5½ oz/150 g cooked chicken, sliced

2 tsp chopped fresh tarragon

1 tbsp chopped fresh parsley

salt and pepper

sprigs of fresh parsley, to garnish

Put the stock in a large saucepan and add the carrots, celery, and leek. Bring to a boil, reduce the heat to low, and simmer gently, partially covered, for 10 minutes.

Stir in the petit pois, rice, and chicken and continue cooking for an additional 10–15 minutes, or until the vegetables are tender.

Add the chopped tarragon and parsley, then taste and adjust the seasoning, adding salt and pepper as needed.

Ladle the soup into warmed bowls, garnish with parsley, and serve.

Chicken Noodle Soup

serves 4–6

2 skinless chicken breasts

5 cups water or chicken stock

3 carrots, peeled and cut into 1/4-inch/5-mm slices

3 oz/85 g vermicelli (or other small noodles)

salt and pepper

fresh tarragon leaves, to garnish

Place the chicken breasts in a large saucepan, add the water, and bring to a simmer. Cook for 25–30 minutes. Skim any foam from the surface, if necessary. Remove the chicken from the stock and keep warm.

Continue to simmer the stock, add the carrots and vermicelli, and cook for 4–5 minutes.

Thinly slice or shred the chicken breasts and place in warmed serving dishes.

Season the soup to taste with salt and pepper and pour over the chicken. Serve immediately garnished with the tarragon.

Chicken & Potato Soup with Bacon

serves 4

1 tbsp butter

2 garlic cloves, chopped

1 onion, sliced

9 oz/250 g smoked lean bacon, chopped

2 large leeks, sliced

2 tbsp all-purpose flour

4 cups chicken stock

1 lb 12 oz/800 g potatoes, chopped

7 oz/200 g skinless chicken breast, chopped

4 tbsp heavy cream

salt and pepper

grilled bacon and sprigs of flat-leaf parsley, to garnish

Melt the butter in a large pan over medium heat. Add the garlic and onion and cook, stirring, for 3 minutes, until slightly softened. Add the chopped bacon and leeks and cook for another 3 minutes, stirring.

In a bowl, mix the flour with enough stock to make a smooth paste and stir it into the pan. Cook, stirring, for 2 minutes. Pour in the remaining stock, then add the potatoes and chicken. Season with salt and pepper. Bring to a boil, then lower the heat and simmer for 25 minutes, until the chicken and potatoes are tender and cooked through.

Stir in the cream and cook for another 2 minutes, then remove from the heat and ladle into serving bowls. Garnish with the cooked bacon and flat-leaf parsley and serve immediately.

Chicken Gumbo Soup

serves 6

2 tbsp olive oil

4 tbsp all-purpose flour

1 onion, finely chopped

1 small green bell pepper, seeded and finely chopped

1 celery stalk, finely chopped

5 cups chicken stock

14 oz/400 g canned chopped tomatoes

3 garlic cloves, finely chopped or crushed

4½ oz/125 g okra, stems removed, cut into ¼-inch/5-mm thick slices

4 tbsp white rice

7 oz/200 g cooked chicken, cubed

4 oz/115 g cooked garlic sausage, sliced or cubed

salt and pepper

Heat the oil in a large, heavy-bottom saucepan over medium-low heat and stir in the flour. Cook for about 15 minutes, stirring occasionally, until the mixture is a rich golden brown.

Add the onion, green bell pepper, and celery and continue cooking for about 10 minutes until the onion softens.

Slowly pour in the stock and bring to a boil, stirring well and scraping the bottom of the pan to mix in the flour. Remove the pan from the heat.

Add the tomatoes and garlic. Stir in the okra and rice and season to taste with salt and pepper. Reduce the heat, cover, and simmer for 20 minutes, or until the okra is tender.

Add the chicken and sausage and continue simmering for about 10 minutes. Taste and adjust the seasoning, if necessary, and ladle into warmed bowls to serve.

Curried Chicken Soup

serves 4–6

- 1/4 cup butter
- 2 onions, chopped
- 1 small turnip, cut into small dice
- 2 carrots, finely sliced
- 1 apple, peeled, cored, and chopped
- 2 tbsp mild curry powder
- 5 cups chicken stock
- juice of 1/2 lemon
- 6 oz/175 g cold cooked chicken, cut into small pieces
- 2 tbsp chopped fresh cilantro, plus extra to garnish
- salt and pepper
- 1/2 cup cooked rice, to serve

Melt the butter in a large saucepan over medium heat, add the onions, and sauté gently, until soft but not brown.

Add the turnip, carrots, and apple and continue to cook for an additional 3–4 minutes.

Stir in the curry powder until the vegetables are well coated, then pour in the stock. Bring to a boil, cover, and simmer for about 45 minutes. Season well with salt and pepper to taste and add the lemon juice.

Transfer the soup to a food processor or blender. Process until smooth and return to the rinsed-out saucepan. Add the chicken and cilantro to the saucepan and heat through.

Place a spoonful of rice in each serving bowl and pour the soup over the top. Garnish with cilantro and serve.

Thai Chicken-Coconut Soup

serves 4

4 oz/115 g dried cellophane noodles

5 cups chicken or vegetable stock

1 lemongrass stalk, crushed

½-inch/1-cm piece fresh ginger, peeled and very finely chopped

2 fresh kaffir lime leaves, thinly sliced

1 fresh red chile, or to taste, seeded and thinly sliced

2 skinless, boneless chicken breasts, thinly sliced

scant 1 cup coconut cream

2 tbsp nam pla (Thai fish sauce)

1 tbsp fresh lime juice

scant ½ cup bean sprouts

4 scallions, green part only, finely sliced

fresh cilantro leaves, to garnish

Soak the dried noodles in a large bowl with enough lukewarm water to cover for 20 minutes, until soft. Alternatively, cook according to the package directions. Drain well and set aside.

Meanwhile, bring the stock to a boil in a large pan over high heat. Lower the heat, add the lemongrass, ginger, lime leaves, and chile and simmer for 5 minutes. Add the chicken and continue simmering for an additional 3 minutes, or until cooked. Stir in the coconut cream, nam pla, and lime juice and continue simmering for 3 minutes. Add the bean sprouts and scallions and simmer for an additional 1 minute. Taste and gradually add extra nam pla or lime juice at this point, if needed. Remove and discard the lemongrass stalk.

Divide the noodles among warmed bowls. Bring the soup back to the boil, then ladle in to each bowl. The heat of the soup will warm the noodles. Garnish with cilantro leaves and serve.

Chicken Ravioli in Tarragon Broth

serves 6

3½ pints/2 litres chicken stock

2 tbsp finely chopped fresh tarragon leaves

freshly grated Parmesan cheese, to serve

for the pasta dough

4½ oz/125 g flour, plus extra if needed

2 tbsp fresh tarragon leaves, stems removed

1 egg

1 egg, separated

1 tsp extra virgin olive oil

2–3 tbsp water

pinch of salt

for the filling

7 oz/200 g cooked chicken, coarsely chopped

½ tsp grated lemon rind

2 tbsp chopped mixed fresh tarragon, chives and parsley

4 tbsp whipping cream

salt and pepper

To make the pasta, combine the flour, tarragon, and salt in a food processor. Beat together the egg, egg yolk, oil and 2 tablespoons of water. With the machine running, pour in the egg mixture and process until it forms a ball. Wrap and chill for at least 30 minutes. Reserve the egg white.

To make the filling, put the chicken, lemon rind and mixed herbs in a food processor and season with salt and pepper. Chop finely, by pulsing; do not overprocess. Scrape into a bowl and stir in the cream. Taste and adjust the seasoning.

Divide the pasta dough in half. Cover one half and roll out the other half on a floured surface as thinly as possible, less than 1.5 mm/1⁄16 inch. Cut out rectangles measuring about 10 x 5 cm/4 x 2 inches.

Place a teaspoon of filling on one half of each rectangle. Brush the edges with egg white and fold in half. Press the edge to seal. Arrange the ravioli on a baking sheet dusted with flour. Repeat with the remaining dough. Allow the ravioli to dry for about 15 minutes or chill for 1–2 hours.

Bring a large quantity of water to the boil. Drop in half of the ravioli and cook for 12–15 minutes, until just tender. Drain on a clean tea towel while cooking the remainder.

Meanwhile, put the stock and tarragon in a large saucepan. Bring to the boil and reduce the heat to bubble very gently. Cover and simmer for about 15 minutes. Add the cooked ravioli and simmer for a further 5 minutes. Ladle into warmed soup bowls to serve with the Parmesan cheese.

Chicken, Mushroom & Barley Soup

serves 4

2¾ oz/75 g pearl barley, rinsed and drained

2 tbsp butter

1 large onion, sliced

1 large leek, trimmed and sliced

4 cups chicken stock

1 lb/450 g skinless chicken breasts, chopped

9 oz/250 g cremini mushrooms, sliced

1 large carrot, peeled and chopped

1 tbsp chopped fresh oregano

1 bay leaf

salt and pepper

sprigs of fresh flat-leaf parsley, to garnish

fresh crusty bread, to serve

Bring a pan of water to a boil. Add the barley and boil over high heat for 5 minutes, skimming the surface when necessary. Remove from the heat and set aside.

Melt the butter in a large pan. Add the onion and cook over medium heat, stirring, for 3 minutes, until slightly softened. Add the leek and cook for another 4 minutes, stirring. Stir in the stock, then drain the barley and add to the pan. Season with salt and pepper. Bring to a boil, then lower the heat and simmer for 45 minutes. Add the chicken, mushrooms, carrot, oregano, and bay leaf. Cook for another 30 minutes.

Remove from the heat and discard the bay leaf. Ladle into serving bowls, garnish with sprigs of fresh flat-leaf parsley, and serve with fresh crusty bread.

Chicken, Leek & Prune Soup

serves 4–6

2 tbsp butter

12 oz/350 g boneless chicken, diced

12 oz/350 g leeks, cut into 1-inch/2.5-cm pieces

5 cups chicken stock

1 bouquet garni

8 pitted prunes, halved

scant 1 cup cooked rice

1 red bell pepper, diced (optional)

salt and white pepper

Melt the butter in a large pan. Add the chicken and leeks and cook for 8 minutes.

Add the chicken stock and bouquet garni to the pan and stir well, then season to taste with salt and pepper. Bring to a boil and let simmer for 45 minutes.

Add the prunes to the pan with the cooked rice and diced bell pepper (if using) and let simmer for 20 minutes.

Remove the bouquet garni from the soup and discard. Ladle into warmed soup bowls and serve immediately.

Chicken & Leek Soup

serves 6

3 lb/1.3 kg chicken

9¼ cups beef stock

2 lb/900 g leeks

1 bouquet garni

1 lb/450 g prunes, pitted and soaked overnight in enough cold water to cover

salt and pepper

Put the chicken, breast-side down, in a large, heavy-bottomed pan or flameproof casserole. Pour in the stock and bring to a boil, skimming off any foam that rises to the surface.

Tie half the leeks together in a bundle with kitchen string and thinly slice the remainder. Add the bundle of leeks to the pan with the bouquet garni and a pinch of salt. Reduce the heat, partially cover, and simmer for 2 hours, or until the chicken is tender.

Remove and discard the bundle of leeks and bouquet garni. Drain the prunes, add them to the pan, and simmer for 20 minutes. Season to taste with salt and pepper and add the sliced leeks. Simmer for an additional 10 minutes. Slice the chicken, or cut into bite-size pieces, and serve.

Turkey Soup with Rice, Mushrooms & Sage

serves 4–5

3 tbsp butter

1 onion, finely chopped

1 celery stalk, finely chopped

25 large fresh sage leaves, finely chopped

4 tbsp all-purpose flour

5 cups turkey or chicken stock

2/3 cup brown rice

9 oz/250 g mushrooms, sliced

7 oz/200 g cooked turkey, diced

3/4 cup heavy cream

salt and pepper

sprigs of fresh sage, to garnish

freshly grated Parmesan cheese, to serve

Melt half the butter in a large saucepan over medium-low heat. Add the onion, celery, and sage and cook for 3–4 minutes, until the onion is softened, stirring frequently. Stir in the flour and continue cooking for 2 minutes.

Slowly add about one quarter of the stock and stir well, scraping the bottom of the pan to mix in the flour. Pour in the remaining stock, stirring to combine completely, and bring just to a boil.

Stir in the rice and season with salt and pepper. Reduce the heat and simmer gently, partially covered, for about 30 minutes until the rice is just tender, stirring occasionally.

Meanwhile, melt the remaining butter in a large skillet over medium heat. Add the mushrooms and season with salt and pepper. Cook for about 8 minutes, until they are golden brown, stirring occasionally at first, then more often after they start to color. Add the mushrooms to the soup.

Add the turkey to the soup and stir in the cream. Continue simmering for about 10 minutes, until heated through. Taste and adjust the seasoning, if necessary. Ladle into warmed bowls, garnish with sage, and serve with Parmesan cheese.

Turkey & Lentil Soup

serves 4

1 tbsp olive oil

1 garlic clove, chopped

1 large onion, chopped

7 oz/200 g mushrooms, sliced

1 red bell pepper, seeded and chopped

6 tomatoes, skinned, seeded, and chopped

generous 4 cups chicken stock

⅔ cup red wine

3 oz/85 g cauliflower florets

1 carrot, peeled and chopped

1 cup red lentils

12 oz/350 g cooked turkey meat, chopped

1 zucchini, trimmed and chopped

1 tbsp shredded fresh basil

fresh basil leaves, to garnish

salt and pepper

thick slices of fresh crusty bread, to serve

Heat the oil in a large pan. Add the garlic and onion and cook over medium heat, stirring, for 3 minutes, until slightly softened. Add the mushrooms, bell pepper, and tomatoes, and cook for another 5 minutes, stirring. Pour in the stock and red wine, then add the cauliflower, carrot, and red lentils. Season with salt and pepper. Bring to a boil, then lower the heat and simmer for 25 minutes, until the vegetables are tender and cooked through.

Add the turkey and zucchini to the pan and cook for 10 minutes. Stir in the shredded basil and cook for another 5 minutes, then remove from the heat and ladle into serving bowls. Garnish with fresh basil leaves and serve with slices of fresh crusty bread.

Turkey, Leek & Bleu Cheese Soup

serves 4

- 4 tbsp butter
- 1 large onion, chopped
- 1 leek, trimmed and sliced
- 11½ oz/325 g cooked turkey meat, sliced
- 2½ cups chicken stock
- 5½ oz/150 g bleu cheese
- ⅔ cup heavy cream
- 1 tbsp chopped fresh tarragon
- pepper
- fresh tarragon leaves and croûtons, to garnish

Melt the butter in a pan over medium heat. Add the onion and cook, stirring, for 4 minutes, until slightly softened. Add the leek and cook for another 3 minutes.

Add the turkey to the pan and pour in the stock. Bring to a boil, then reduce the heat and simmer gently, stirring occasionally, for about 15 minutes. Remove from the heat and let cool a little.

Transfer half of the soup into a food processor and blend until smooth. Return the mixture to the pan with the rest of the soup, stir in the bleu cheese, cream, and tarragon and season with pepper. Reheat gently, stirring. Remove from the heat, ladle into warmed soup bowls, garnish with tarragon and croûtons and serve.

Lemon Turkey Soup with Mushrooms

serves 4

- 12 oz/350 g boneless turkey, cut into ½-inch/1-cm pieces
- 4 cups chicken stock
- 1 onion, quartered
- 2 carrots, thinly sliced
- 2 garlic cloves, halved
- 1 pared strip lemon rind
- 1 bay leaf
- 1 tbsp butter
- 12 oz/350 g small button mushrooms, quartered
- 4 tbsp cornstarch
- ½ cup heavy cream
- freshly grated nutmeg
- fresh lemon juice, to taste (optional)
- 1–2 tbsp chopped fresh parsley
- salt and pepper

Put the turkey in a large saucepan and add the stock. Bring just to a boil and skim off any foam that rises to the surface.

Add the onion, carrots, garlic, lemon rind, and bay leaf. Season with salt and pepper. Reduce the heat and simmer, partially covered, for about 45 minutes, stirring occasionally, until the turkey is cooked.

Remove the turkey and carrots with a slotted spoon and reserve, covered. Strain the stock into a clean saucepan. Discard the onion, garlic, lemon rind, and bay leaf.

Melt the butter in a skillet over medium-high heat. Add the mushrooms, season, and cook gently until lightly golden. Reserve with the turkey and carrots.

Mix together the cornstarch and cream. Bring the cooking liquid just to a boil and whisk in the cream mixture. Boil very gently for 2–3 minutes until it thickens, whisking almost constantly.

Add the reserved meat and vegetables to the soup and simmer over low heat for about 5 minutes until heated through. Taste and adjust the seasoning, adding nutmeg and a squeeze of lemon juice, if using. Stir in the parsley, then ladle into warmed bowls and serve.

Asian Duck Broth

serves 4–6

2 duck leg quarters, skinned

4 cups water

2½ cups chicken stock

1-inch/2.5-cm piece fresh ginger

1 large carrot, sliced

1 onion, sliced

1 leek, sliced

3 garlic cloves, crushed

1 tsp black peppercorns

2 tbsp soy sauce, or to taste

1 small carrot, cut into thin strips or slivers

1 small leek, cut into thin strips or slivers

3½ oz/100 g shiitake mushrooms, thinly sliced

1 oz/25 g watercress leaves

salt and pepper

Put the duck in a large saucepan with the water. Bring just to a boil and skim off the foam that rises to the surface. Add the stock, ginger, carrot, onion, leek, garlic, peppercorns, and soy sauce. Reduce the heat and simmer, partially covered, for 1½ hours.

Remove the duck from the stock and set aside. When the duck is cool enough to handle, remove the meat from the bones and slice thinly or shred into bite-sized pieces, discarding any fat.

Strain the stock and press the vegetables with the back of a spoon to extract all the liquid. Remove as much fat as possible. Discard the vegetables and herbs.

Bring the stock just to a boil in a clean saucepan and add the strips of carrot and leek, the mushrooms, and duck meat. Reduce the heat and cook gently for 5 minutes, or until the carrot is just tender.

Stir in the watercress and continue simmering for 1–2 minutes until it is wilted. Taste the soup and adjust the seasoning if needed, adding a little more soy sauce if desired. Ladle the soup into warmed bowls and serve immediately.

Duck Soup with Scallions

serves 4

2 duck breasts, skin on

2 tbsp red curry paste

2 tbsp vegetable or peanut oil

bunch of scallions, chopped

2 garlic cloves, crushed

2-inch/5-cm piece fresh ginger, grated

2 carrots, thinly sliced

1 red bell pepper, seeded and cut into strips

4 cups chicken stock

2 tbsp sweet chili sauce

3–4 tbsp Thai soy sauce

14 oz/400 g canned straw mushrooms, drained

Slash the skin of the duck 3 or 4 times with a sharp knife and rub in the curry paste. Cook the duck breasts, skin-side down, in a wok or skillet over high heat for 2–3 minutes. Turn over, reduce the heat, and cook for an additional 3–4 minutes, until cooked through. Lift out and slice thickly. Set aside and keep warm.

Meanwhile, heat the oil in a wok or large skillet and stir-fry half the scallions, the garlic, ginger, carrots, and red bell pepper for 2–3 minutes. Pour in the stock and add the chili sauce, soy sauce, and mushrooms. Bring to a boil, reduce the heat, and simmer for 4–5 minutes.

Ladle the soup into warmed bowls, top with the duck slices, and garnish with the remaining scallions. Serve immediately.

Asian Chicken Meatballs & Greens in Broth

serves 6

8 cups chicken stock

3 oz/85 g shiitake mushrooms, thinly sliced

6 oz/175 g bok choy or other Asian greens, sliced into thin ribbons

6 scallions, finely sliced

salt and pepper

for the chicken balls

1 oz/25 g chicken, minced

1 oz/25 g fresh spinach leaves, finely chopped

2 scallions, finely chopped

1 garlic clove, very finely chopped

pinch of Chinese 5-spice powder

1 tsp soy sauce

To make the chicken balls, put the chicken, spinach, scallions, and garlic in a bowl. Add the 5-spice powder and soy sauce and mix until combined.

Shape the chicken mixture into 24 meatballs. Place them in one layer in a steamer that will fit over the top of a saucepan.

Bring the stock just to a boil in a saucepan that will accommodate the steamer. Regulate the heat so that the liquid bubbles gently. Add the mushrooms to the stock and place the steamer, covered, on top of the pan. Steam for 10 minutes. Remove the steamer and set aside on a plate.

Add the bok choy and scallions to the pan and cook gently in the stock for 3–4 minutes, or until the leaves are wilted. Taste the soup and adjust the seasoning, if necessary.

Divide the chicken meatballs evenly among warmed bowls and ladle the soup over them. Serve immediately.